# THE LOVE SONG OF SAUL ALINSKY

*An Entertainment in Two Acts
Based on His Life*

by
Herb Schapiro

FOUNDED 1830
New York  Hollywood  London  Toronto
SAMUELFRENCH.COM

Copyright © 2007 by Herb Schapiro

*ALL RIGHTS RESERVED*

*CAUTION: Professionals and amateurs are hereby warned that THE LOVE SONG SAUL ALINSKY is subject to a royalty. It is fully protected under the copyright laws of the United States of America, the British Commonwealth, including Canada, and all other countries of the Copyright Union. All rights, including professional, amateur, motion picture, recitation, lecturing, public reading, radio broadcasting, television and the rights of translation into foreign languages are strictly reserved. In its present form the play is dedicated to the reading public only.*

*The amateur live stage performance rights to THE LOVE SONG SAUL ALINSKY are controlled exclusively by Samuel French, Inc., and royalty arrangements and licenses must be secured well in advance of presentation. PLEASE NOTE that amateur royalty fees are set upon application in accordance with your producing circumstances. When applying for a royalty quotation and license please give us the number of performances intended, dates of production, your seating capacity and admission fee. Royalties are payable one week before the opening performance of the play to Samuel French, Inc., at 45 W. 25th Street, New York, NY 10010 or to Samuel French (Canada), Ltd., 100 Lombard Street, Lower Level, Toronto, Ontario, Canada M5C 1M3.*

*Royalty of the required amount must be paid whether the play is presented for charity or gain and whether or not admission is charged.*

*Stock royalty quoted upon application to Samuel French, Inc.*

*For all other rights than those stipulated above, apply to Samuel French, Inc., 45 W. 25th Street, New York, NY 10010.*

*Particular emphasis is laid on the question of amateur or professional readings, permission and terms for which must be secured in writing from Samuel French, Inc.*

*Copying from this book in whole or in part is strictly forbidden by law, and the right of performance is not transferable.*

*Whenever the play is produced the following notice must appear on all programs, printing and advertising for the play: "Produced by special arrangement with Samuel French, Inc."*

*Due authorship credit must be given on all programs, printing and advertising for the play.*

ISBN **978-0-573-65129-8**     Printed in U.S.A.     #13771

| No one shall commit or authorize any act or omission by which the copyright of, or the right to copyright, this play may be impaired. |
|---|
| No one shall make any changes in this play for the purpose of production. |
| Publication of this play does not imply availability for performance. Both amateurs and professionals considering a production are strongly advised in their own interests to apply to Samuel French, Inc., for written permission before starting rehearsals, advertising, or booking a theatre. |
| No part of this book may be reproduced, stored in a retrieval system, or transmitted in any form, by any means, now known or yet to be invented, including mechanical, electronic, photocopying, recording, videotaping, or otherwise, without the prior written permission of the publisher. |

## IMPORTANT BILLING AND CREDIT REQUIREMENTS

All producers of THE LOVE SONG OF SAUL ALINSKY *must* give credit to the Author of the Play in all programs distributed in connection with performances of the Play, and in all instances in which the title of the Play appears for the purposes of advertising, publicizing or otherwise exploiting the Play and /or a production. The name of the Author *must* appear on a separate line on which no other name appears, immediately following the title and *must* appear in size of type not less than fifty percent of the size of the title type.

**SAUL ALINSKY (1909-1972)**
Organizer • Gadfly • Performer on the American Scene

"He is twice formidable, and very close
to being an organizational genius."
— William F. Buckley, Jr.

"Alinsky is truly radical…
he actually believes in democracy."
— Adlai Stevenson

"He is one of the few truly great men
of this century."
— Jacques Maritain

"The Establishment can accept being screwed,
but not being laughed at. What bugs them
about me is that, unlike the humorless radicals,
I have a helluva good time doing what I'm doing."
— Saul Alinsky

# ACKNOWLEDGEMENTS

In his personal mission for over thirty-five years, as an organizer for native Americans, minority groups, college students, and the middle class, among others., in numerous encounters, demonstrations, lectures, and impromptu talks, Alinsky would often refer to some of the same favorite experiences and the illustrations they offered. Versions of these accounts, from a variety of sources, would then find their way into his own two books, Reveille for Radicals and Rules for Radicals, a range of magazines, from Playboy to Harper's, as well as the recent biography by Sanford D. Horwitt, many interviews and more informal sources.

In drawing on certain of these episodes here, I have attempted wherever possible to offer them in Alinsky's own words, often after consultation with Dr. Irene McInnis, Alinsky's wife and colleague, whose first-hand knowledge, understanding and bracing wit have been a constant guide and inspiration throughout the development of this work.

The ultimate acknowledgement is to the man himself, whose bravery, candor and selfless dedication to people and the true meaning of democracy remain a fresh and often entertaining alternative to their opposites today.

## The PEOPLE

Saul Alinsky
Associates of Alinsky—Jose, Martha, Hattie, Jack—
who assume varying roles

## The TIME
1972…Only Yesterday

## ACT I: The Activist Alone

Scene — A motel somewhere in the middle of America, Alinsky on a bad night late in his career, alone with his memories, reveries, fantasies.

The room is angular, suggested rather than constructed, more a frame than a literal representation, the door off-center towards stage right, rear; the whole on a slight platform where ALINSKY will move from the present into playing areas of the past and of fantasy.

In some productions, such a "set" might be replaced by a bare stage, with projections now providing a sense of scene as we move from the '20s through the '60s, and possibly commenting on portions of the action. Incidental music may also help create the particular atmosphere of individual sequences, and of memory itself.

## ACT II: The Activist and His Audience

Scene — The next day, the audience in our theater now becoming Alinsky's own audience, the action played more directly to them, as people come to hear what he has to tell them, to show them.

Where Act I moves with the flow of associations, as a set of free variations on several themes, Act II is improvisational in style, for these are performers on the scene who have been here many times before, with audiences of one kind or another.

## ACT I

## The Motel
### *Somewhere in America. 1972.*

*(At the outset, VOICES from without, mingling with, then overcoming, the sound of period pop, news, commercial bits, on a radio.)*

**VOICES.**
"Who the hell are you, anyway, mister?"
"Whaddaya doin' here?"
"We don't need no outside agitators here…"

*(A cigarette lit, and light up on ALINSKY, the room all plastic and chintz.)*

"Why doncha go the hell back where you came from, Alinsky?"

**ALINSKY.** Ah, fame, those siren voices calling…My welcoming committee…

*(VOICES continue under ad lib, begin to fade.)*

**VOICES.**
"Yeah, who the hell needs you here?"
"Go home. How 'bout cleaning up your own house?"
**ALINSKY.** Good questions…
**VOICE.** "Hey, Alinsky, ya been 'organizin'—what?—25, 30 years — Chicago, KC, LA…all over…"
**ALINSKY.** A scholar, one in every crowd…Yeah, all over…
*And it's 3 A.M.*
*You're all alone.*

*A cheap motel.*
*And there's no phone.*

*You say your piece, you keep your word,*
*They want to hear, but no one heard.*

*And you look away and wonder*
*When the mirror gives you back*
*Those lines that trace an unfamiliar map*
*On a face you once knew…*

And tomorrow? What the hell do I give them tomorrow?

**VOICE.** "So why doncha take a break? Do somethin' different—organize yourself…somewhere else.

*(Echo: "…back where you came from.")*

**ALINSKY.** Where the hell <u>do</u> I come from? Chicago? Mama? Poland? Pithecanthropus Alinskyensis—organizer

of the first cavemen's  association against the sabre-toothed cavelords? Where did I go wrong?
**VOICE.** "…back where you came from, Jack."
**ALINSKY.** What was I, 10 . . . 11?

*(Voices fade, light up downstage right, ALINSKY moving through frame, joining MARTHA, as his MOTHER there.)*

**MOTHER.** "Whoever hoid of such a ting?"
**ALINSKY.** "I told ya, ma—my best fren' was beat up by some of the Polish kids, so we just crossed over and…"
**MOTHER.** "The disgrace…the way you were raised…"
**ALINSKY.** "We beat the bejesus out of them, that's all. They started…"
**MOTHER.** "To drag your own mother to the station house— what am I, a well person? I should promise the sergeant…the Irish…we'll take care of you when we get home?"
**ALINSKY.** With that kind of protective custody, who needed jail?
**MOTHER.** "I'll show *you*, mister—*this* is where you're going, to the *rabbi!"*

(*Pulls him by the ear, leads him to JACK, as RABBI here.*)

**RABBI.** "When…when will you learn to deny the iniquity which is there in your heart, sonny? When will you cease visiting shame upon your blessed mother, which gave you birth amidst the affliction of her body? Can not you tell from wrong what is what, a person of your age, look at you, no child?"
**ALINSKY.** "Look, rabbi—it says so right in the Bible, you said it: 'an eye for an eye, a tooth for a tooth.' They give me

a black eye, I give them one. And besides, it's the American way, to fight back. So we beat the hell out of them. That's what everybody does, what they all do, isn't it?"

**RABBI.** *(Long pause, and...)* "You tink you're a man because you do what everybody else does? No. No, sonny boy. Let me tell you something the great Rabbi Hillel said about this, and you should remember it, so listen, listen...hear...'Where there are no men...be *thou* a man.' You hear, you understand? You don't forget: 'Be *thou* a man. Moses, Moses was a man, a *mensch*. You be, too.'

*(Fade on RABBI, ALINSKY slowly crossing back through frame and into motel room.)*

**ALINSKY.** I still hear it, old man. Keep the faith. *(He picks up Gideon Bible, thumbs through it idly.)* Bible lessons, hah? Let my people go...back where they came from...Hmm... How did Moses do it, anyway? Must have been one helluvan organizer, coming up against his people, coming up against... the Establishment of Establishments, eh?

*(Begin FANTASY SEQUENCE.)*

**VOICE.** *(HATTIE as The LORD.)* "I am the Lord, thy God. There shall be no other gods before me. What's the story with these people, anyway? I'm a jealous and vindictive God, they know it. And they turn around and worship...what? this Golden Calf? After they were Chosen, special, they were told this, after they knew they were supposed to play it by The Book, an instrument of truth, a light among nations? Who in Heaven's name do they think they are? How much patience do they think I have? They expect me to act like Job? No, no. I don't need to, I don't have to. I raised them up and I can drop them, like a poor relation. These people have to go. Let them wander around in the desert till they find themselves. Enough. That's *it.*"

**JOSE.** "Maybe we can go up, talk it out. We do have a relationship…We did it before. Maybe something like this… 'Lord, they're not really bad people, just going through a phase. We can straighten it out. Why not give 'em a break, another chance, that kind of thing?'

**GOD.** "Go, get thee down. Thy people brought out of the land of Egypt hath sinned."

**MARTHA.** "Where's Moses?

*(ALINSKY forward, as MOSES.)*

**MOSES.** "I don't think we want to make a pitch for justice or mercy. That's all *they* hear…'We lost our heads. We didn't mean it. Give us a break.' No. We don't want to beg. And we don't want to lose our cool. Not our style here. Won't work."

**GOD.** "I am the Lord, thy God. There shall be no other gods before me."

**MOSES.** "There. You hear that? That tells me something, the important thing here…to be Number One. You get it over and over again into the Commandments. A preoccupation. And when you suggest there may be a threat to it, a crisis, *then* they listen."

**JACK.** "Yeah, maybe you've been out in the desert sun too long.. I mean, just how would you "negotiate" with Number One?"

**MOSES.** "Maybe something like this… 'Lord, no one has to tell you you're holding all the cards. For God's sakes, you can do whatever you want. Who's going to stop you? Who in his right mind would even attempt to cross you?' Like that, maybe. You start some kind of dialogue, you try to disarm the other guy. "Let's see. Yes…The Covenant. That's it… 'Lord, forgive me, but you remember the Covenant—you handled the negotiations, you promised to take them out of slavery, you guaranteed they'd inherit the earth, all of that. Well, there's a problem—you made a deal, with all respect. And now you want to scratch it. I know, I know, they broke their end of it. Sure they did. But it isn't that easy. I mean, we're a little closer to the scene here, and it looks like—no disrespect intended—you're in a spot.'

**GOD.** "How…in God's name, in the name of the Almighty, man…!"

**MOSES.** "Well, there's been a leak, that's how. News of the deal is all over the place. Everybody knows about it—the Egyptians, the Philistines, the Canaanites…you name it. *Everybody.* But you're the Supreme One. Of course, you're right. By definition. What do you care if people all over are going to say 'There goes the Almighty, the Lord of Hosts. Number One. And you can't believe a thing he tells you. His word isn't worth the stone it's written on.'"

**GOD.** *(After a long pause.)* "And the Lord was appeased from doing the evil which had been spoken against the people."

**ALINSKY.** Now that's organization for you…
I always say you have to identify with your people…

*(End FANTASY SEQUENCE.)*

**VOICES.**
"There's no free lunch, buddy."
"Get the hell outta here…"
"Go the hell back where you came from…"

**ALINSKY.** 'You can take the boy out of Chicago, but you can't take…' City of the Big Shoulders and the Bigger Mouths. Hog Butcher for the world…run by the Hogs themselves Capone, Kelly, the meatpackers…Ah, yes…

**VOICE.**
"Get lost, punk…"

**ALINSKY.** Can't get shut of those voices. Heard 'em since…school days…and ever after. Hmm…never thought of it that way before but maybe majoring in…archaeology at the university…*archaeology!*…maybe I was thinking it was one way to get out of Chicago…But there was that Aztec altar at the museum, great place…stone and clay…funny the way it crosses my mind now. Lessons for the young activist, the kid organizer…Stand before it, close your eyes, feel those strange vibrations coming at you…and then hear the cries of the victims, flesh and blood, of all those sacrifices. (*Long pause…*) Must remember to mention it…work it in tomorrow…

**VOICES.**
"Get lost…Go 'round the corner and see if the sun's shining."
"Beat it the hell outta here…an' don' come back…"

*(Segue to INVESTIGATION SEQUENCE.)*

**JACK.** (As INVESTIGATOR) "Mr. Alinsky, would you tell the committee how you came to be regarded as a 'subversive menace'— a 'public enemy of law and order,' according to the Chicago Tribune — as early as your college days."

**ALINSKY.** "What can I say? I own up to it. I could tread the straight and narrow no longer. I went wrong."

**INVESTIGATOR.** "Could you be more specific about these…irregularities?"

**ALINSKY.** "Let's see…It all started with the college cafeteria caper. '29…'30. Yeah, I graduated in 1930…with a major in archaeology."

**INVESTIGATOR.** " 'Archaeology?' "

**ALINSKY.** "That's right. You know, digging into things. Something we have in common. But it wasn't a good year for archaeological expeditions…or for eating, as I remember it. I used to go into one of those 'deluxe' food shops where they always gave out free samples—ham and cheese, you know. And junket at the dessert counter—'Junket'—great name… they still sell that? Or is it just something they associate with Congressmen, politicians, now. Another kind of free lunch."

**INVESTIGATOR.** "Could you focus only on the bare facts, please?"

**ALINSKY.** "The 'bare facts,' yes. Oh, yes—*eating.* Anyway, after a month of junkets, two guys came up to me in the middle of a mouthful and threw me out."

**VOICES.**
"Stay out, dammit."
"So here you are, such a smart sonuvabitch—*cum laude* and all that, and you can't make a living."
"Yeah, how come?"

**ALINSKY.** "It's called The Great Depression now. Then it was only very depressing. I was having a cup of bad coffee in one of those chain restaurants, and thinking. And I began to hear voices…"

**INVESTIGATOR.** "'Voices?'"

**ALINSKY.** "Yeah. I guess I was hungry. Then I remember—I took my coffee, sat down next to the cashier, and started chatting with her. And then, I guess I got ready to go… 'Oh, Jeez—I can't seem to find my check. I'm sorry. Guess I must have lost it somewhere.'"

**HATTIE.** (*As CASHIER. Pause)* 'Well all you had was a cup of coffee, right? That'll be a nickel.'

**ALINSKY.** "She gave me a check and I paid that one, then I walked a few blocks to another restaurant in the same chain, with the original check in my pocket, had myself a meal—for, maybe, a buck fifty-five…that was *eating* in those days—and paid for it all with the five-cent check. Ahh…"

**INVESTIGATOR.** "So it was at that point that you were running afoul of the law."

**ALINSKY.** "I confess. It pained me. But my hunger pains were greater. I mean, in my defense, it's hard being a useful member of society on an empty stomach. I was getting like that Jean Valjean in *Les Miserables.* Yeah, I guess it got worse…"

**INVESTIGATOR.** "Oh? The committee would be especially interested in that phase of your career, as a possible lesson to others similarly inclined."

**ALINSKY.** "My conscience started to bother me. All around the university there were kids as hungry as I was. I just couldn't keep my terrible secret to myself."

**INVESTIGATOR.** "You formed something of a gang then?"

**ALINSKY.** "I made up some signs and posted them around the campus"…

**JOSE.** *(As student, reading aloud.)* "Fellow Students… These are the times that try our souls and deny our stomachs. If you are among those both hungry for learning and concerned about where your next meal is coming from, you are invited to a discussion of a new system for keeping body and soul together through regular eating during the current crisis…"

"It's gotta be a gag…"

**ALINSKY.** "They came out, anyway. I had a big map of Chicago, with all the chain restaurants starred. I explained my system. Soon I organized teams, for the North Side one day, the South Side the next. I saw it as a practical use of social ecology: you had members of the intellectual community, the hope of the future, eating regularly for six months, staying alive till they could make their contributions to society."
**INVESTIGATOR.** "Just the facts. What then?"
**ALINSKY.** "Well, automation finished us off: check machines. You had to take one good only for that place."
**VOICE/JOSE.** "What the hell are we gonna do now? We count on you and you let us down."
**INVESTIGATOR.** "Wasn't there a *'criminal element'* you became involved with at that time?"
**ALINSKY.** "'Criminal element?' Well, let's see—I suppose you can call it that, if you consider the Capone gang as a 'criminal element.'"
**INVESTIGATOR.** "Excuse me?"
**ALINSKY.** "Oh, you wouldn't remember, young fella—no disrespect intended—but our own Big Al *was* the Establishment. Before he became a 'criminal element.' The operation was run as a kind of quasi-public utility. Let me explain. It supplied whatever the people wanted. Strictly business, supply and demand. Some babes…?"
**INVESTIGATOR.** "You refer to… *women*?"

**ALINSKY.** "Of the night, yes. But you could have 'em any time. Supply. Demand. Booze? No problem—and you could work up a real thirst during Prohibition. Talk about organization! My, my…Action at the track? Sure thing. Business was very good, as you probably heard. And everyone owned stock in the operation—Capone was like a public benefactor…"

*(In b.g., crowd noise, first dim, then building in next moments.)*

**INVESTIGATOR.** "The committee is concerned with your own connection. Please."
**COMPANY.** "Yea, yea. Big Al! Yea, yea, Big Al…"

*(Continuing under.)*

**ALINSKY.** "Yes, yes, of course. I think I first felt the lure of the mob when Big Al showed up at a Northwestern football game…on Boy Scout Day. Yes, that was it—the place went wild, thousands of fans just rose up as one and started cheering. It was inspirational…*(Chant, cheer, up and fade.)* You felt you wanted to be a part of it. I mean, all those leaders of tomorrow… and all that character-building. And other entrepreneurs like Roger Touhy and Bugs Moran—you heard of these big guns, on tv, right?—they wanted in, business was so good. When one of the boys suffered 'an accident,' there wasn't a court in session: the judges were all at the funeral—no disrespect intended— paying their respects, and some of them were pallbearers. It was natural to want to be close to them all, the power structure, the organization. To feel, well, *connected.*"
**INVESTIGATOR.** "Yes. And . . .*your* participation? Go on. Yes?"

**ALINSKY.** "No. Come to think back, it wasn't really the Northwestern game that set me on the ol' primrose path. I remember now: it was the University itself you could say pushed me into becoming a member of the gang."

**INVESTIGATOR.** "You're not suggesting the University of Chicago was involved in...?"

**ALINSKY.** "Yeah, that was it. Of course. It started with a letter I got one hungry morning from the President himself, that's right—awarding me a graduate fellowship...in criminology."

**INVESTIGATOR.** " 'You did say 'criminology?' "

**ALINSKY.** "It all made sense. I hadn't taken one course in it, and all I knew about it was what I learned in the cafeterias. Maybe they were trying to reclaim me from my drifting into the 'criminal element.' There was full tuition, room and board, and...I tell ya, I weakened. A life preserver and a meal ticket in the middle of the Depression. And in a way I'd have a chance to get closer to the heroes of Chicago. For a kid from the streets, what could be bad? I made my move...then it happened."

**INVESTIGATOR.** "Your real introduction to the underworld..."

**ALINSKY.** "I found out that criminology had as much to do with crime as...some investigations have to do with truth. So I decided to go out in the field and do my own dissertation on the Capone gang. That's right. An inside study. That's where the action was."

**INVESTIGATOR.** "So, according to your testimony, it was at that point that you became, as you say, 'connected' and that had its effect on your organizing career."

**ALINSKY.** "What could I do? They waltzed into my life and seduced me with their...*savoir-faire* and the lure of success..."

*(Fade on INVESTIGATOR, segue to BIG AL SEQUENCE. COMPANY with cigars, fedoras and canes, a strutting CHORUS of CAPONES.)*

### SONG: *"CAKEWALK FOR CAPONES"*

**COMPANY.**
WE GOT THE STUFF
CAN'T GET ENOUGH
YEAH YEAH YEAH YEAH
ANYTHING GOES

JUST WIPE YOUR NOSE
JUST KEEP IT CLEAN
KNOW WHAT I MEAN
YEAH YEAH YEAH YEAH

SO WHADDAYA KNOW
'N WHADDAYASAY
LOOK OUT BELOW
GET OUTTA DA WAY

AIN'T IT A SHAME
JUST PLAY DA GAME
YEAH YEAH YEAH YEAH
WE GOT IT MADE
JOIN THE PARADE
YEAH YEAH YEAH YEAH

*(And over to downstage playing area, now the HOTEL HEADQUARTERS of The Mob, ALINSKY as grad student, recognizing them, "connecting.")*

**ALINSKY.** "Say there, I'm Saul Alinsky...studying criminology over at the university. Wonder , would you mind if I just hung around with you guys for a while?"
**JOSE.** (*As mobster.*) "Get lost, punk."

*(ALINSKY fades to side, moping...when another joins mob at table.)*

**ALINSKY.** *(Aside)* "Jeez, the Lord High Executioner himself, Big Ed Stash..."
**JACK.** *(As STASH.)* "Hey, you guys—did I ever tell yez about that redhead in Detroit, da one with the mother had an eye for Big Ed...?"
**JOSE.** "Crissakes, Ed, do we gotta hear that one again?"

*(STASH sinks from the rebuff, as ALINSKY moves in, touches his sleeve.)*

**ALINSKY.** "Say, Mr. Stash, I never heard that one. I'd really love to hear you tell it."
**STASH.** "You would, kid? Hey, come on over here. Yeah, pull up a chair. *(Ad lib under, and...)* Wha...? Sure. Come aroun,' *anytime...*"
**ALINSKY.** Archaeology...criminology...and then the Capone College for Social Organization...*(Laughing)* under Frank Nitti himself...*(And into scene now, JOSE as NITTI.)* "Professor, there's something here I don't get."
**NITTI.** "You college kids got all kinds a' problems, ain't ya?"
**ALINSKY.** "Well, I was looking into the books, and I see somethin' strange..."

**NITTI.** "What the hell does that mean?"

**ALINSKY.** "Well, I'm lookin' at a $7500 payment for an out-of-town enforcer."

**NITTI.** "Yeah? Ya gotta pay him for his work. So…?"

**ALINSKY.** "What I don't get is why you bring in a guy from St. Louis and pay him these bucks when you got twenty guys on the payroll can just do the job, like that. Doesn't seem very efficient to me."

**NITTI.** "Kid, kid…kid—what the hell do they teach ya in dose schools, anyway? All right, listen good. So ya get a good mark on the test, hah? "Look, sometimes *our* guy might *know* the guy he's gonna hit, ya unnerstan'? Might 'a been to the house for dinner, taken his kids to see the White Sox, might 'a been best man at the weddin', gotten drunk together…Ya get the picture? Think it over, genius…"OK. But ya call in another guy from out-a-town, there's no problem--all ya gotta do is tell 'im: 'Hey, there's this guy in a dark coat corner State Street. Our boy in da car'll point 'im out. Ya go up feed 'im t'ree in da belly, an' fade wid da wind. "Now, ya see kid—he's a pro, he moves right in, no questions, that's it, that's a *job*. But ya send in one of *our* boys, the guy toins ta face 'im, and…Jeez, it's a fren', right away he knows he pulls the trigger, there's gonna be a widow, kids widout a fodder, funerals, bawlin', all 'a that—dontcha see it?—Christ, it'd be *moider!*"

(*He shakes his head, as he fades to the side.*)

**ALINSKY.** It wasn't The Untouchables…but it was long-running, with reruns. And it was "moider" all right. Right in the tradition…"Moider" Incorporated, the Memorial Day Massacre…dozens of pickets done in…the Chicago police riot. A look back to the '30s and you see the attempted murder of The Dream—from Boss Kelly back then to Deadeye Dick Daley and the Demo-Critic Convention in '68…Stays with you, all of it. Follows you everywhere, right to this chintz outhouse. Have to write about it…

**VOICE / MARTHA.** *(As WIFE.)* "I don't know if this will reach you, Saul—you don't stand still long enough for any mailman to catch up with you. But I'll take the chance—that's the way it is with us, isn't it? This way If the mail gets to you, somehow, you could at least carry it around with you. When we speak on the phone, sometimes I don't know if you're really there, if you're not somewhere else. What I mean is that I seem to know you more as a voice at the end of a wonderful invention—I love the magic of it, but I don't see *you*. So fold me, put me in your pocket, carry me with you. It's *something*… "I have the usual trouble—what do I tell the kids? 'Well, he's like a traveling salesman, sort of?' Somehow that doesn't do it. 'Daddy's a crusader, like a knight in shining armor, and that takes him away—on business?' I don't know, they just shrug. 'He's a soldier, yes, at the frontlines…in a war that just seems to go on and on—but he'll be back.' He'll be back. They really ask the damnedest questions."

**ALINSKY.** And so you're always going to be late to dinner. And Thanksgiving.

**VOICES.**
"Go back where you came from."
"Put your own house in order."
"What are you, some kind of Polish joke?"
"Polish *jerk.*"

"You people can't let well enough alone, can ya?"

"Stay with your own kind."

"The poor . . . always with us . . ."

"Brother, can you spare a. . ." ". . . Dream . . . I have a . . ."

"Threat to public safety . . ." "Always with us . . ."

"Point of order, point of order . . ."

"CAN YOU SPARE SOME...CHANGE ...some change... ?"

### ALINSKY.
*(A kind of improvised sprechstimme.)*
*My country . . . 'tis of whatthehell*
*And justice up a tree . . .*
*How much can you sell*
*What's in it for me*
*Hey who can't be bought*
*And why is that smell*
*Neighbor*
*Comin' from you*
*We'll see ya in court*
*So what else is new*
*O say can't you see past your nose*
*A new world*

### VOICES.
"That stink, man—that's my whole life . . ."
"Stays with you . . ."
"Hey, go fight City Hall...Got my check, maybe I hit the

numbers, do a li'l hustlin' . . ."

"Raise kids? For what? To grow up next to the slaughterhouse, let 'em feel they're next?"

"Cash it in—the whole damn thing . . ."

"Goddam bastards . . ."

*(Segue to COLLEGE REPORTER INTERVIEW.)*

    **ALINSKY.** "…What was that line...? *Shakespeare*... Funny . . .*never* was over here, never knew the stockyards, Chicago, Depression, the rest of it: 'Lilies that fester . . .smell far worse than weeds.' Nice line, hah?"
    **REPORTER.** *(JACK)* "Let's see. That was Chicago, the area known as Back of the Yards."
    **ALINSKY.** "That was a lot of places—Kansas City, Oakland, Rochester . . ."
    **REPORTER.** "How did you get started there, Mr. Alinsky? How did you manage to get things organized? The kids on campus will be very much interested in reading about it—you know, with the war in Viet Nam and the demonstrations going on?"
    **ALINSKY.** "Well, I was about your age, so I was still very idealistic. 'Are you now, or have you ever been, an idealist, or a member of any organization that advocated . . .'"
    **REPORTER.** "Sir?"
    **ALINSKY.** "Nothing. Just got carried away. OK. There was a lot of work to be done, anyone could see that, although most were looking the other way. And work was a good antidote

to despair, right? ...Was it Voltaire who said something like... If you don't want to commit suicide, get to work. Anyway, I went in and asked questions. As you might say, I "identified." Say, have you ever seen those Aztec artifacts in the Chicago Museum? Go some time. Not too far from the old stockyards. Very moving."

**REPORTER.** " Yes?"

**ALINSKY** "You made them feel they were not alone, others felt the same way, and there were some who really cared—you can't fake that. I talked, I listened, listened some more, asked more questions. I learned. So when you heard some of them saying, We don't need your kind, or Who ast ya to come here, you could answer, Hey, *you* did—it became agitation by invitation. They *wanted* me there. "I was pushing my own New Deal, I guess, and the idea was there was a way out of that jungle—same one Upton Sinclair wrote about...turn of the century...same rot, same corruption, our stockyards. Read about it in class?...Well, the meatpackers and the papers got all worked up about what we were doing; I was no longer a crazy sonuvabitch—I was upgraded to "public menace," a "threat to law and order." It was a real promotion. Get the picture?"

**REPORTER.** "They tried to close you down, shut you up. What happened then?"

**ALINSKY.** "It worked—for us. And better than we expected."

**REPORTER.** "Could you . . . clarify that? I don't know if our readers . . ."

**ALINSKY.** "Kid...kid—what do they teach you in those schools? Just think about it...they're making a big fuss, carrying on, going public about this Alinsky clown doing such terrible things, tearing the fabric of our common welfare, stuff like that.

Meanwhile I'm working with the people, who have the truth right under their nose, and to them it smells like this Alinsky guy can't be all bad, must be OK to get those bastards all worked up, maybe has somethin' on 'em, or else they wouldn't be so worried. "A form of psychological jiu-jitsu—you use the strength of the Establishment—especially the press—against itself, get it? You get them to commit with what they have and what they know, in a way that has to be, for them, counter-productive. Think about it—they have all that machinery, all that reinforcement—their own Fort Knox...you have your slingshot and your *imagination.* So you work with what you have and stop bitching about what you lack." *(Aside to himself.)* Good to remember that...now, in this plastic palace...Yeah, out there in the Depression with our wits and no base but what we were sitting on...and we didn't sit very often. Couldn't. Flies from the stockyards would suck us dry...

**REPORTER.** "You had the support of the Catholic church, Mr. Alinsky?"

**ALINSKY.** "We *earned* the support of the church. We needed a base, and Back of the Yards was roughly 100% Catholic, so we learned to speak their language to enlist them in the cause."

**REPORTER.** "The appeal to conscience and morality, that idea . . ."

**ALINSKY.** "The appeal to experience and the collection plate—and an answer for the universal question: What's in it for us?"

**REPORTER.** "The Sermon on the Mount, brotherhood . . .?"

**ALINSKY.** "They heard it all, over and over again. No. We talked about how their congregations are starving for bread and butter and signing up with the 'bad guys,' the 'Communist unions,' the action groups…We talked about how the church has to beat them at their own game, show the flock the priests are more concerned about living conditions, bread and butter, than they are about business as usual. "The flock comes back—they know you're on their side, you stand up for them—and when they win something, they're grateful for it—donations, involvement in the life of the church," that kind of thing...We talk their language and they become 'activist,' in their own way, and soon we're holding organizational meetings in their churches. We're not out in the cold knocking on doors, but inside, getting ready to fight City Hall."

**REPORTER.** "So in a way it was now '*Onward, Christian Soldiers*,' and you were their captain."

**ALINSKY.** "Yeah, you could say that...I kind of like that."

**REPORTER.** "And now you were marching on City Hall and Mayor Daley..."

**ALINSKY.** "There you go again. Jeez, you college kids these days…This was the '*30s*—there was life before Daley, in a manner of speaking, and Boss Kelly was its name. Actually, Kelly made the Daley machine look like the League of Women Voters. Like a club, the ABA— Associated Bosses of America. Pendergast in KC, Hague in Jersey City, Mayor Curley in Boston—you gotta keep a warm spot in your heart for a mayor working his re-election campaign from his jail cell."

**REPORTER.** "I remember my grandmother saying she voted for him."

**ALINSKY.** "We're a forgiving people…You know, they delivered the votes for the Democrats, and when FDR had to deal with them, he's have 'em sneaked in through the back door of the White House. The truth…Say, is this like school to you?…Anyway, Kelly, Kelly was something special. Capone looked better to the public than he did. He was, you might say, anti-social, Kelly was…like the part he played in the Memorial Day Massacre—union demonstrators killed by the police. 'Put the bastards down'—that was a fair statement of his social philosophy. But he had his finer sensibilities…like Capone and Frank Nitti…You know these guys, right?—You watch television."

**REPORTER.** "You're not talking about Howdy Doody."

**ALINSKY.** "That's right. And not The Honeymooners either."

**REPORTER.** "The 'finer sensibilities' you mentioned . . ?"

**ALINSKY.** "Ah, yes—the quest for respectability. Work as a full-time thug but be recognized as a pillar of the community. Noble aspiration. Nothing hurt Kelly more than the way he had to use the back door to the White House…He really admired FDR, worshipped him even—in spite of his own, say, skepticism, about labor and unions and people who had to work for other people, and anyone who didn't have any power. He felt rejected—'the back door, please'—and no invites to the dinner parties or the Sunday soirees Eleanor used to throw. Ah, rejection is a terrible thing, sometimes scars you for life, turns you into a monster. Who couldn't identify with a guy like that? Sad, very sad…after all the work he'd done for the cause, and…"

*(Fade in last moments on REPORTER, as ALINSKY segues into office of Mayor KELLY…)*

**JOSE.** *(As KELLY.)* "Whaddaya got to deal with, kid?"

**ALINSKY.** "Look, your Honor, I know I can't deliver any more votes than you already got... "*(Aside)* Jeez—they didn't bother to count the votes in those days, they weighed them... and every cemetery in Chicago turned out for the big elections ... "But I'm gonna deal with you, that's why I'm here." *(Aside)* Just out of graduate school, and what *cojones* I had...

**KELLY.** " 'Deal,' hah? Sure...with *what,* kid?"

**ALINSKY.** "Look, I think you're a man who appreciates straight talk. And you're a man who appreciates some of the... better things in life…"

**KELLY.** "What was that? Who the hell said so?"

**ALINSKY.** "Well, in any case, right now, with the common man, with labor, millions out there striving for a fair share of the American pie…"

**KELLY.** "Slice it, will ya? I'm a busy man. How the hell'd you get in here anyway?"

**ALINSKY.** "Straight talk, hah?...Well, with them, you're Public Enemy Number One."

**KELLY.** "That's supposed to be some kinda news flash?"

**ALINSKY.** "The point is the whole country knows it, but I can *change* all that. Yeah. I can deliver the endorsement of the CIO and the support of every union in Chicago."

**KELLY.** "Come on, *talk* to me. Talk to me."

**ALINSKY.** "OK. Let me lay it out. I got two guys who were wounded in the Massacre. I can arrange for them to go on radio and talk about Mayor Kelly, the only true friend of the working man. That's right. I mean, within 24 hours you'll be transformed completely into a champion of liberalism."

**KELLY.** "That's *it*? *That*? You gotta be kidding."

**ALINSKY.** "Hold on. When that happens, in no time at all, for instance, you'll be walking through the front door of . . . the White House, things like that."

**KELLY.** "How do I know you can deliver?"

**ALINSKY.** "How? Here...here's the number of John L. Lewis in Alexandria. Unlisted. Yeah, *that* John L. Lewis—the High Priest of Pickets. I worked with him when he first started organizing for the union. Go ahead. Call him up. He'll be glad to hear from you. Tell him I'm in your office, let him know what I said, and ask *him* if I can deliver. Go ahead, do it now while you can. You're a busy man."

**KELLY.** "Whaddaya want, kid?"

**ALINSKY.** "I know we can talk man-to-man, right. Let me be candid with you, Your Honor."

**KELLY.** "Yeah. You be candid."

**ALINSKY.** "I want you to put the screws on the meatpackers, get 'em to sign a contract with the union. That's all. No baloney. That's it."

**KELLY.** *(Pause)* "You got it. You can pick up the papers in 24 hours."

*(Fade on KELLY, light up on REPORTER...to him, ALINSKY.)*

**REPORTER.** "Would you say that *organizing* makes strange bedfellows, Mr. A.?"

**ALINSKY.** "I would say that playing charades can be a profitable pastime...with real prizes for your team—jobs they can work at, housing they can live in...rent they can pay... garbage they're sure will be picked up...schools they can send their kids to and have *them* learn some of the good things and grow up without knowing their neighborhood was one of the worst in the country. You know, air you can breathe without

choking, right? It ain't nirvana, kid, just a way out of the jungle ...if somehow you play it right."
**REPORTER.** "I can see that, yes...Do you mind if some of the other kids come by to talk with you?"

*(Fade on REPORTER sequence, segue to ...)*

**ALINSKY.** *(To himself again, very much in the motel.)* What it comes down to...always have to feel there's some place to go...feel you're going *somewhere*. . . .Yeah, sure—come by ...talk to me...
**VOICE/MARTHA.**
*(In sprechstimme, as WIFE.)*

"Where are you...?
*I never know what's right or fair*
*I only ask how can I care*
*And where*
*Where are you*

*For just one time*
*I'd like to do the things*
*That other people do,*
*But where are you?*
*Why not come home*
*Just for a break*
*Share a breath*
*What does it take*
*No matter what you do or dare*
*All that will wait for you out there*

*Do I seem cold*
*Am I unkind*
*You lose some hair*
*I lose my mind*

At least the people have a prayer when you are there…

*I do not know what's right or fair*
*I only ask why should I care*

*And how could I ever leave you dear*
*If you are never here."*

*(Segue to Kansas City Sequence, JOSE as POLICE OFFICER.)*

**OFFICER.** "OK, fella, let's go to the station house where it's nice and quiet and you'll be good and safe."

**ALINSKY.** "You reading me my rights?"

**OFFICER.** "You'll get a chance to catch your breath, movin' around the way you do, makin' trouble. Must take a lot out of you."

**ALINSKY.** "Keeps you guys working, anyway, so I guess we're in this together, hah?...But say, do you think I might be released in the protective custody of my mother?"

**OFFICER.** "Smart guy. We heard about what you're doin' in Detroit, California, other places. The war's over…and we don't need no trouble here in Kansas City."

**ALINSKY.** "They told me you did—church people, some of your neighborhood organizations. Asked me to manage it."

**OFFICER.** "Don't know anything about that, but you'll be comfortable here. No one'll bother you."

**ALINSKY.** "Yeah, a home away from home…Say, you know, I've got some important friends in Chicago might wonder what kind of treatment I'm getting. You heard of Marshall Field…the Third? And the Bishop of Chicago? They're behind me in this…my associates."

**OFFICER.** "Sure, and I'm J. Edgar Hoover."

**ALINSKY.** "Nah. C'mon—I *know* J. Edgar Hoover. Sends his Boy Scouts to see that I take my vitamins. By the way, what's the charge?"

**OFFICER.** "For the accommodations? No charge. 'Bishop of Chicago'—you guys are really somethin.'"

**ALINSKY.** "Call him up, why don't you . . .But say, man-to-man, what am I in for?"

**OFFICER.** "They're working on it at the office. Public nuisance. Disturbing the peace…that kind of thing. You qualify…Can't be too careful these days. The Commies are everywhere."

**ALINSKY.** "That too, hah? Well, let's see—can I get a pencil and some paper, along with my bread and water?"

**OFFICER.** "Can't see why not—it's a free country."

*(Fades to side.)*

**ALINSKY.** A good place to relax, collect some thoughts. Better than this damn motel…KC was like that. Good service, decent help…upstanding.

**VOICES.**
"Hey, if this Alinsky guy cares enough about us to go to the pokey, we can't let him down."

"You know he's got somethin' to say—otherwise they wouldn't

bother with him."

**ALINSKY.** Yeah, and good to get off the road . . . *for a break.* Build expectation.They put you away for a stretch the people forget about you…same as they could if you're lost in this retirement home for too long…

**OFFICER.** *(Returning)* "You been our guest for a few hours now. Captain says he's sorry to see you go, but he knows you got these pressing engagements to attend to. Says he'll probably see you later on."

**ALINSKY.** "I'd rather not go…just yet. I'd like to finish the chapter I'm working on."

**OFFICER.** "You writin' about us? A bit uppity for a jailbird, aren't you? We can clip your wings, if you'd like."

**ALINSKY.** "I'm serious, man. Don't get a chance out there on the road to stop and take stock."

**OFFICER.** "And reform your ways?"

**ALINSKY.** "Well, somebody's, anyway. Nice place you have here. Better than the others I've been to."

**OFFICER.** "Thanks. A home away from home, hah? But why don't you just go back where you come from – Chicago, isn't it? *Real* problems there."

**ALINSKY.** "Same problems. Same people. But I know you have a job to do. I understand. I used to work in a state prison. That's right. Joliet. State criminologist. For a while. Studied it in college…Yeah, true. You can look it up…Then I went straight."

**OFFICER.** "You know, I could almost believe you. Maybe we'll talk some time."

**ALINSKY.** "Sure. I'll probably be back, one time or another."

**OFFICER.** "You're a little different from our usual clients, you know...?"

**ALINSKY.** "It's all surface…" (*OFFICER to side, fade and segue to*...) So important to make friends when you're out on the road..."

**VOICE/JACK.** "Though the hour be late in this emergency session of the City Council of our fair city by the Bay, I should like to amend the motion to ban this Alinsky and his motley crew, and propose in addition, in the name of the city of Oakland itself, that we send this instigator, this outside agitator, this un-American rabble rouser, a 50-foot length of heavy duty rope, along with the recommendation that he use it...to 'suspend' his indecent activities... "

**MARTHA.** *(As TV REPORTER.)* "You've heard the proposal of the Oakland City Council, sir…"

**ALINSKY.** "Yes. We've already sent our response—a box of disposable diapers. Jumbo-size."

**REPORTER.** "I see. You are aware that the Chief of Police has announced that the threat you present to the public safety will be . . . 'neutralized' at the Oakland city limits, by 'any and all available means.' Can you comment on that statement?"

**ALINSKY.** "Yes. Of course. We plan to join forces with our brother and sister radicals of the Presbyterian Church on the other side of the water. They have sent for us in their hour of need. We cannot turn a deaf ear to their cries for social justice."

**REPORTER.** "Can you divulge anything of your strategy, for the benefit of our audience and the community who've been following this story from the first announcement of your intention to come to Oakland, anything at all?"

**ALINSKY.** "Yes. We expect to march across the Bay Bridge with a contingent of anywhere from ten to...twenty

Americans. I will be in the fore-front. I will be armed..."
**REPORTER.** "Oh?"
**ALINSKY.** "...armed with my birth certificate in one hand, and my passport in the other. We look forward to seeing you and your audience there, of course. 'We shall meet the enemy—and the enemy may be us." Happy times. Nice memory. And nice coverage to help things along. Ah, the uses of the status quo, now and forever. And so much fun when they really get to know you...

*(Segue to McCARTHY and FANTASY SEQUENCE.)*

**VOICE/McCARTHY.** *(Dimly, in background, the drone, over and over.)* "Point of order...point of order...point of order...!"
**JOSE.** "The year 1952 in the Eternal Struggle of Us Versus Them...The Honorable Joseph R. McCarthy and his sponsors invite your participation in a new extravaganza, with full TV coverage, based on the Spanish Inquisition, the Salem Witch trials, and the Conflict between Civil Rights and Civil ...Wrongs."
**JACK.** *(As McCARTHY.)* "You're subpoenaed to appear: how do you plead?"
**JOSE.** "You're expected to name names—fellow travelers, dupes of the Commies, Red agitators—and join in the public confession of your sins against us."
**ALINSKY.** A command performance...before The Mother of All Senatorial Investigations into the Behavior of The Bad Guys—how could you refuse? Everyone was there, when you think back—Cotton Mather, Hester Prynne, Anne Hutchinson, Tom Paine, Tom Jefferson...Brandeis, Holmes...Gene Debs

and the socialists…Huey Long…Imperial Wizards of all stripes …Father Coughlin and his money machine...Daffy Duck, Elmer Fudd . . . and a kicking chorus of sterilized reactionaries singing O Come, All Ye Faithful...

**VOICES.**
"Are you now . . ?" "Could you be . . ?"
"Who was there . . ?" "Did you see . . ?"

**ALINSKY.** Step right up and see, right before your very eyes—magicians transforming old friends into pigeons, enemies into sheep and goats…and Congressmen into jackasses…

**VOICES.**
"Point of order…point of order…point of order…"
"Was he there . . .?" "Did she know . . ?"
"When they left . . ?" "Did you go . . ?"
"Have you been . . ?" "Are you now . . ?"
"There are ways . . ." "Tell us how . . "

**ALINSKY.** For the land's sakes—isn't that, among the clowns and acrobats—yes, it's...Cotton Mather...Scourge of the Unpuritan, walking on fire and brimstone!

**VOICE.** Give 'em hell!

**ALINSKY.** P.T. Barnum…

**VOICE.** Good show! There's a sucker born every minute, so go get 'em, bring 'em to justice. This way to the egress, folks.

**ALINSKY.** And, yes—the most venerable Elmer Fudd...

**VOICE.** Ooh, *thoth wascals!*

**McCARTHY.** "Point of order . . . point of order! . . .Point of information . . ."

**VOICES.**
"Are you now…?" "Have you ever…?"
"Will you tell…?" "Now or never…"

**McCARTHY.** "Mr…Alinsky…that it? Odd name..I'm making a list…checking. it twice—gonna find out who's naughty…with vice…"We have petitioned your cooperation in this critical investigative enterprise, in the name of the good and loyal people of America…doing, as Mr. Lincoln said, for the people what the people cannot…or will not, or are too lazy to do for themselves…and that labor symbolized by this flag, these stars and stripes, that I proudly wear. "The committee expects your full cooperation, Mr….Alinsky?...Hmm …uncommon name—*Eastern* European origin, isn't it? Your performance before us, Mr. Minsky, will be duly recorded for the benefit of the American people who wish to know your part in the subversive activities sponsored by the Reds in Moscow. In brief, your reputation will be on the line, Mack."

**ALINSKY.** *(Wild laughter, echoes, and a drum roll.)* " 'Reputation? Reputation?' *What* reputation?"

**McCARTHY.** "Point of order . . . point of . . . departure!"

**ALINSKY.** "I call for the defense the distinguished member of the clergy, the Reverend Charles Lutwidge Dodson..."

**McCARTHY.** (*Aside*) "Is he on our list?"

**ALINSKY.** "He is not able to attend these proceedings today due to a popular indisposition, but will be represented by his assistant, Miss Alice."

**VOICE.**
"They told me you had been to her, And mentioned me to him; She gave me a good character, But said I could not swim . . ."

**ALINSKY.** "Thank you for your testimony. Regarding the possible redundancy of these proceedings, I now call to the stand—the Right Honorable Lord High Executioner of Titipu."

**VOICE.** "As some day it may happen that a victim must be found, I've got a little list—I've got a little list Of society offenders who might well be underground, And who never would be missed—who never would be missed!"

**McCARTHY.** " 'List? List?' Point of…"

**ALINSKY.** "The esteemed market researcher and spokesman for the American Dream, Mr. Thomas Paine…"

**VOICE.** "Let them call me rebel, and welcome—I feel no concern from it; but I should suffer the misery of devils, were I to make a whore of my soul."

**McCARTHY.** "We'll have no case made here for whores and devils. Do we have his name on the list? Point of information…"

**ALINSKY.** "A final witness, Your Honor, Your Jury, Your Justice—a prepared statement from the representative from Missouri, the 'Show Me' State, the retired pilot of his own ship of state, Captain Mark Twain."

**McCARTHY.** (*Aside*) "That name…clearly an alias…"

**VOICE/TWAIN.** "Will the day come when the race will detect the funniness of these juvenilities and laugh at them—and, by laughing at them, destroy them? Against the assault of laughter nothing can stand. Power, money, persuasion, supplication, persecution—these can lift at a colossal humbug…"

**McCARTHY.** "Point of order…the witness will refrain from making oblique scurrilous references or threats to particular individuals."

**VOICE/TWAIN.** *(Continuing)* "…at a colossal humbug, push it, weaken it a little,
 century by century, but only *laughter* can blow it to rags and atoms at a blast. But who uses it? Who has the sense, and the outrage?"

**ALINSKY.** "Laughter in the court!"

**McCARTHY.** "Order, dammit! We will tolerate no innuendoes not certified by the committee. Have you anything more to say before your fate is determined by your superiors? That is, mend your speech lest you mar your goddam future."

**ALINSKY.** (*After a pause.*) "No laughter...no innuendoes. That's tough, really unfair. But I will cooperate. I'll tell you all I know...(*tremolo...drum roll.*) about your own acrobatics against Bob LaFollette, back in '46, when you scrambled for support from the local Commies, and yes, some of the latest about your *extra*—Congressional relations, and..."

**McCARTHY.** "Point of...What's the point of all this goddam scuttlebutt!"

**ALINSKY.** "The point, dear Brutus, is not in our stars: a lot of our problems come about because we neglect to say, to the wrong people, at the right time—Just who the hell do you think you are, anyway?"

*(Echoes here, drowning out the drone, and segue to...)*

**VOICE.** (*In the Bill Buckleyan mode.*) "Could you share with our studio auditors—and those citizens enjoying this miracle from the electron tube in the sanctity of their domiciles... your thoughts on the following observation in a recent issue of the venerable TIME magazine: 'Alinsky's work in organization is, at bottom, based on bedrock cynicism.'"

**ALINSKY.** "Apparently another venerable typographical error. Should be 'bedrock *realism.*' Some people are always confusing the two."

**VOICE/BUCKLEY.** "Ah, but when you say— as I believe you do—of our church leaders that the Sermon on the Mount does not speak to their direct experience, are you not expressing a certain cynicism regarding some of the most cherished beliefs of our people?"

**ALINSKY.** "Help me here—was it Aquinas who wrote about the mind and the need to make distinctions? I believe, in what you seem to be referring to, we spoke of the relationship of bread and butter to the progress of the soul, the body being the temple of the spirit. Of course, the church leaders you mention recognized the connection, and the realism that characterized our discussion, and we both worked well, I think—in the interests of 'our people.'

**VOICE/BUCKLEY.** "Have you, then, studied the writings of the Church Fathers?"

**ALINSKY.** "I've had my Bible lessons. You know, there's one passage especially—in the New Testament—comes to mind every so often…"

**VOICE/BUCKLEY.** "Yes?"

**ALINSKY.** "I'm sure you're familiar with it—the one where the…speaker…says: 'I am come not to destroy, but to fulfill.' I find that very creative, and inspiring."

**VOICE/BUCKLEY.** "I see. Tell us, can you, in these attempts to achieve your, shall we say, '*fulfillment*…to maximize the leverage of the disenfranchised, the disadvantaged, and, may I add, with a sense of culmination and crescendo, the *discontented*—do you recognize any *failures,* their relevant causation, do you see any…?"

*(VOICE fades, continuing under, and out.)*

**ALINSKY.** These 'wretched, rash, intruding fools…' Failures? Failures? Only every goddam day. The damn despair at doing anything at all…Inertia, suspicion, distrust waiting to meet you at every turn, kick you in the groin. 'Let it alone, let it rot?' Getting too old for this, need these kneecaps intact, can't afford to get hit on the head much more. 'Any failures?" Just the normal ones, and the successes—of a Sisyphus from Chicago, pushing uphill against the odds. Well, it's the push upward against the dead weight of things that counts, isn't it, fella?—not the fact the damn load you shoulder can overwhelm and bury you any time you try to catch your breath. And all the time the ones you leave behind, the ones who ask you to just catch your breath once in a while…'Fold me, carry me with you . . .What do I tell the kids?'

**VOICE.** "Saul, get some rest, guy. They say there'll be a good crowd."

**ALINSKY.** "Yeah, yeah . . ." And tomorrow is another day…

*(Echoed by VOICES/COMPANY as we move into sprechstimme.)*

**ALINSKY.** *SO WHAT THE HELL.   WHAT'S THERE TO SAY*
**VOICES.**
       And how do you do.    And why are you here
       and what can you say  At 3 a.m. In a cheap motel.
       West of milwaukee     Or east of l.a.

**ALINSKY.** *NEAR THE COUNTY SEAT OF WHATTHEHELL.*
**VOICES.**
       But tomorrow is another day

**ALINSKY.** *AND SOME THEY SHOUT TO HAVE THEIR SAY*
          *WHILE OTHERS SMILE    THEN TURN AWAY*

**MARTHA.** "Try the TV            try not to think"

**JOSE.**       "What's on the tube      What's there to drink"

**MARTHA.** "Why not come home    Just take a break
                 Stop for a while         What does it take"

**ALINSKY.** *IT'S HALF-PAST THREE*
               *AND NOT MUCH LIGHT*
               *SO HOW WAS YOUR DAY*
               *AND WHO'LL SAY GOOD NIGHT*

**VOICES.**
"Hey, you O.K., Saul?"
"Don't wanna make us come and get you." *(laughter)*

*(ALINSKY starts for a moment: Could these be some of the local hired goons—or just some of his own people mimicking them, fooling around?)*

"Shut the light and get some rest, will ya?"

**ALINSKY.** *YEAH IT'S VERY LATE     WHAT MORE TO SAY*
             *THAN TOMORROW IS     ANOTHER DAY*
             *AND MAYBE THINGS MAY STILL GO WELL*
             *AND IF THEY SAY THERE'S HELL TO PAY*
             *WHAT CAN WE DO       BUT GIVE 'EM HELL*

*(Laughter, and fade on room.)*

**THE LOVE SONG OF SAUL ALINSKY**

## ACT II

## The Meeting
## Next day.

*(COMPANY on stage of auditorium as ALINSKY joins them, prepares to address audience, nothing anxious or tentative in his manner. The occasion is there, and he will rise to it; clearly welcoming their presence, he is "on.".)*

**ALINSKY.** You know, I was thinking just before about some things our good friend Mark Twain had to say about us. Said first, we didn't laugh enough. Wasn't his fault, right? Thought we didn't have the guts to ridicule the twits and thugs who handle our war and bigotry programs, and our money-changing. And for me, what I've seen is that the Establishment can accept being screwed, over and over, but not being laughed at. Think about it. What bugs them most about me is that I'm a little different from the humorless radicals—I have a helluva good time doing what I'm doing...And sometimes maybe it means we may all have a better time together, tomorrow. So I thought we'd share some of our recent happy adventures with you—my All-American gypsies who've been with me in the field and down the road, on my mind and in my heart. They'll help me get organized one more time…and maybe you'll get into the act. Let's see—have you heard the one about Mayor Daley?

**HATTIE.** "Mr. Mayor, regarding the rights demonstrations and the war in Viet Nam, could you give us your own feelings about the divisions among our people?"

**JOSE.** *(As DALEY here.)* "I don't see it, I tell ya. There are no more serious divisions in the country than we had in the Civil War…and some other times."

**ALINSKY.** It was always hard to place Dick Daley in any of the great philosophical traditions.

**JACK.** "Sir, during the recent marches, the police apparently arrested many peaceful demonstrators, while ignoring those who were throwing rocks and eggs at them and trying to break through the police lines. Would you agree with the officials who made that decision, in apparent violation of the rights of the demonstrators?"

**DALEY.** "The captain told me the only way to keep the peace was to lock up those who were peaceful. Think about it.. The onlookers were disorderly—we knew that—and if our men started arresting them, well, they might start a riot. I can understand that."

**JACK.** "I see, yes."

**DALEY.** "I think we pay too much attention to these things in the press. Today, if you ask me, the real problem is the future."

**HATTIE.** "Would you say that was the problem with the Woodlawn community here in '64?"

**DALEY.** "'Problem?' What kind of problem?" (*Fussing, fuming, then, aside . . .*) Give 'em an inch an' they take an ell…

*(What the hell's an ell, anyway?)* Sometimes you just gotta tell 'em to get the 'ell outta there, what I say. I mean, so they built up the neighborhood, with this Alinsky jerk, they got in the way of the developers and the University people, stood 'em off, started all that crap about doin' their own urban renewal program, doin' their own thing like those damn hippies . . . so what do they want—a citation, the goddam Nobel prize? 'Yeah, I told 'em I'd come in for somethin'—so what? Who the hell needs 'em? They don't vote anyway. What are they gonna do, go for Goldwater, all of a sudden? LBJ'll run away with it, so what the hell's the fuss? I'll deliver without 'em...'

**HATTIE.** "Mr. Mayor, were there any commitments made by your administration to the community organization?"

**DALEY.** "No comment..." *(Aside)* Always have to give ya a hard time, that crowd, make your job difficult. I mean, it's a bitch – how long do I have to listen to that crap? Whatever you do for them, it's never enough, for crissakes. A load of crap...'

**ALINSKY.** A down-to-earth type guy, a man of the common people, a man who understands basic functions...

**DALEY.** (*Aside*) 'Who the hell's behind them, anyway—the Commies, or those goddam Republicans?'

**ALINSKY.** And a man of aspirations, seeking his monument after years in the public eye...ear, nose, craw...A man, you might say, now with his head in the clouds...

**JOSE.** *(As HIMSELF.)* Huh?

**ALINSKY.** O'Hare Airport, for instance—His Honor's pride and joy, international gateway to the heart of America, symbol of the vision and enlightenment of his venerable administration...Chicago big on progress, squarely on that map, unlimited visibility. And if anything, anything at all went wrong at O'Hare...

**DALEY.** "I'll have their asses, dammit!"

**ALINSKY.** Well, there was something wrong at Woodlawn, and then there was O'Hare, the pride and joy, perfection itself, and the idea was to bring the two together somehow, and see if we could make it fly. A kind of Chicago flight plan, for those who have been grounded too long. O.K. Let's see—we always figure tactics is doing what you can with what you have.

**MARTHA.** No money.

**JACK.** No influence, that kind of thing.

**ALINSKY.** Pity? No. What we did have was people--many warm, concerned bodies in that community—and also something else we often forget we have: imagination, our wits, and, maybe, a sense of humor about even the things that oppress. So…we have the first sketches of our 'flight plan.' Say you're a passenger on a flight to O'Hare. You've had a drink and something to eat, perhaps accompanied by some turbulence and heavy vibrations. Chances are your thoughts will soon be turning to some even more basic functions. But your problem has a problem: you can't move for the people next to you and the trays which have to be collected.

**JOSE.** I always get an aisle seat. Foresight.

**JACK.** When it's all clear, the ones who are closest get to our little comfort station in the sky and we're reading the OCCUPIED signs.

**HATTIE.** *(As FLIGHT ATTENDANT.)* "Attention, please. Your captain asks that you return to your seats at this time and fasten your seat belts. To minimize any inconven-ience regarding the use of the sanitation facilities, your captain suggests you adopt a comfortable posture, with legs pressed together, and engage in deep rhythmic breathing and meditation exercises. You may also find it helpful to visualize pleasant experiences you have had in your recent travels with us . . . "

**JOSE.** You're breathing, and it's April in Paris... 'holiday tables under the trees...' *(Humming the song here.)*

**HATTIE.** *(Continuing)* "Your attention, please. We are now beginning our descent into...your seats in an upright position."

**JACK.** "Well, it won't be too long now, and the rest rooms at O'Hare have to be luxurious in comparison to this doll house outhouse."

**ALINSKY.** All a matter of research. Exit polls: your plane lands and 57% of the passengers find the johns to be the most popular place to visit. The more sociological studies indicate that anxiety, associated with baggage repossession and connection-linkage, will often increase the sense of urgency to 63%.

**MARTHA.** It's beginning to come together. The plot. The tactics.

**ALINSKY.** The game: Let's say at flight arrival times we simply occupy all the comfort stations—we have the occupation forces ready to mobilize—and the man in the City Hall control tower knows it. All those visitors to O'Hare looking forward to Daley's pride and joy, amenities, state-of-the-art progress, and what do they find?

**JACK.** A major variation on the sit-in . . .

**HATTIE.** And Chicago's most up-to-the-moment kind of relief program...

**ALINSKY.** Crowds milling about, shifting uneasily from side to side, trying to look cool, mumbling as they double up, and cursing O'Hare, Chicago, the Boss himself, whose idea of progress failed to include the most basic human conveniences.

**JOSE.** *(As MAYOR DALEY.)* "What the hell's goin' on over there, dammit? Everything's backed up—I'll have their asses!"

**JACK.** We were set to make his kind of music—a Windy City Symphony for Big Brass and assorted Ill Winds.

**MARTHA.** Or maybe, a chamber opera—"The Discomforts of Daley," or "Daley Undone . . ."
(*Improvising*)
O HOW FAR HAVE I GONE
TO FIND YOU DEAR JOHN
AND NOW AT LAST I SEE
THAT YOU ARE HERE
BUT WHO ARE THEY
INSTEAD OF ME
AHEAD OF ME
O JOHN
HOW I COULD CRY
NOW THAT I SEE
JUST HOW FAR GONE
FROM YOU AM I

**ALINSKY.** We figured it wouldn't run long. It didn't have to. Just enough to make it memorable. Chicago loves a good show, something like the adventure of Mrs. O'Leary's cow. And it would get the headlines, and the reviews, in all the papers—local, all over--with TV coverage . . But maybe…all that might be unnecessary, even if it was to be fun, if we invited to our strategy session a double agent, a well-known informer working for the administration…to leak the news beforehand . . . I believe that's the expression. I guess it was a tactic I learned from the Old Pretender, Joe McCarthy himself. Remember? Made quite a name for himself, in the dictionary, too. The one who also taught us that power is not only what you have, but what the other guy thinks you have. Was that the phone I heard?

**MARTHA.** *("Answering the call")* "'From the Mayor's office…' Yes. "'There seems to be a rumor circulating around town…' Uh-huh…'a demonstration to take place at O'Hare… some miscommunication problem.' You say the Mayor would 'like to meet tomorrow morning with…' Yes, yes… 'Woodlawn Organization representatives, to clarify any misunder-standings.' Well, that certainly is news. And we'll certainly relay this information to the right people. Yes. Someone will be back in touch with your office. Yes. We have your number, yes.'"

**ALINSKY.** Handshakes. Good will. Concessions. And it wasn't even Christmas, or Election Day. Everyone was relieved—I think that's the expression. You know, later on, one of our people heard Daley say, "That guy, Alinsky—he loves Chicago, same as me." You don't have to spread it around. My reputation, you know.

**MARTHA.** What did you expect? You speak his language.

**JACK.** You use the same washrooms.

**ALINSKY.** Guess we just went to different schools.

**JOSE.** Ah, it's all about education, isn't it? Getting down to the fundamentals…

**HATTIE.** Building on them for a better future, a real foundation, changing things for the better…

**JOSE.** Like that fundamentalist college on the last lecture tour, for instance?

*(Laughter, and segue into COLLEGE SCENE.)*

**JOSE.** "Mr. Alinsky, sir, we here enjoyed your talk on… 'Happy Strategies for Effecting Social Change.'"

**JACK.** "Took a lot of notes. A lot there, sir . . ."
**MARTHA.** "Thought about what you said. Discussed it all."
**JACK.** "You see, we're concerned."
**HATTIE.** "Problems, problems all the time . . . "
**JOSE.** "Tryin' to find our way through the strait and narrow. Sometimes it just gets too hard, sir. Can't talk to them about it. Maybe you might give us an idea, if you will."
**JACK.** "Mr. Alinsky, what it comes to—they treat us like kids. Plain and simple. Don't let us smoke . . .
**JOSE.** "Don't let us drink beer . . ."
**MARTHA.** "No dancin' allowed. Anything like that."
**JACK.** "Can't party. Nothin' . . ."
**HATTIE.** " Nothin' ...That's not livin'."

*(Echoes, ad libs.)*

**ALINSKY**. " 'Nothin', you say. You're sure? Nothing? Isn't there anything they let you do that you feel you should be able to do? Anything?"

*(Confusion, caucus, and . . .)*

**JOSE.** "Yeah. There's somethin'. I guess they let us chew gum. They don't say anything anyway. So what? Big deal."
**ALINSKY.** "Just a minute. Let's examine this a little more closely."
**JACK.** "Bubble gum, Chiclets, gum balls, sticks—spearmint, peppermint . . . "
**HATTIE.** "Tutti-frutti . . ."
**ALINSKY.** "Yeah. OK. Now you're thinking."

**JOSE.** "Huh?"

**ALINSKY.** "Well, we always say, Tactics is doing what you can—with what you've got. You feel powerless, can't do anything? Stop and take an inventory. See what you do have, and then think about how you can use it. Chewing gum, hah? That's it? Plus your imagination—can't forget that. So, I assume you have access to your sources of supply, you can get all you need, right? No problem there. And your moral imagination is intact, while the administration lacks empathy, basic human feeling, plain consideration of your reasonable needs. That's the picture. OK…"

**JACK.** "Could you go a little slower, sir, so I can get all this down?"

**ALINSKY.** "Right. Well, what are the special properties of chewing gum, say, when you cram five or ten sticks in your mouth and go chewing for broke? And then deposit the messy wad, let's just say in a strategic place, where it might get some attention from the right people, let 'em know you're here and you need to be counted in, reckoned with? Don't you see— Gum is your secret weapon in the revolutionary struggle!"

**JACK.** "Wait a minute. You mean…?"

**ALINSKY.** "Look. I'm from Chicago. Now, if there were, say, five hundred people there, like yourselves—disenfranchised, disadvantaged, disregarded— *(Not too farfetched when you think of it.)*—those five hundred jaws could create five hundred roadblocks to tie up the city, stop all the traffic, and the shopping, in the Loop, and let everyone at City Hall know attention must be paid, and maybe we should talk about it. O.K.? All clear? Send me a progress report at general headquarters." The college kids these days—what do they teach 'em in those schools, anyway? But they learn, they learn, even though it may take a while.

**HATTIE.** *("Reading")* "Dear Mr. Alinsky, "Following our conversation a few weeks ago, we had several strategy sessions with our student government representatives. We would like to inform you that we seem to have discovered how to 'effect change' in our society. In effect, we created a "sticky situation"—you might say we "gummed up the works." The deans called us in soon after to discuss our grievances and see if we could come up with a new student Bill of Rights. "The atmosphere is a lot freer now. The upshot is that we now can smoke, we can drink beer, in moderation. We are now permitted to have dances. We can have parties. Coed. Other things. And we want to thank you for your guidance in our darker hours. "Actually, there's only one thing, one catch-- we're absolutely forbidden to chew gum. Well, it's a sacrifice, all right, but we thought we could concede on that one, and you would agree . . ."

*(Ad libs, and segue back.)*

**ALINSKY.** What's really depressing is the fact they never realized the answer was there, at the tip of their tongues. Students of the world, unite! You have nothing to lose but your Juicy Fruit! It was an experience, being back in college after all those years. Thirty...thirty-five years ago, between classes, we were conspiring to get us something to eat. I was speaking at a big university not long ago—let me share this with you. There the students were sensitized to causes and programs and crusades...everything from pure foods and free love to bad wars and ghettos, and worse politicians. Every so often, during a break, I was taken back to the '30s—to John L. Lewis organizing for labor when management had lost its way...and to the war—then the Spanish Civil War to make the world safe for Fascism—and for Hitler…and Father Coughlin on the radio preying on his millions of listeners every week to send in more money to make the world safe for bigotry. And some of us who were trying to work at some kind of New Deal all the while. I remember getting back to the hotel late, about one-thirty or so, and stopping off at the bar for something to ease the transition. There was only the barkeep, mopping up, and, down at the other end, a Marine in dress uniform, master sergeant, hash marks up and down his sleeve, lots of salad on his chest, campaign after campaign, year after year, the kind they call "strapping," the kind you'd like on your side in a fight. And he was crying. He'd seen the worst and here he was, crying.

**JACK.** *(As BARTENDER.)* "I don't know what it is, but he's been at it for hours, and belting them down like gangbusters, like there's no tomorrow. Sobbing and crying. Just like that. I don't think it's a woman. I don't know, a big guy like that. I'd like to get out of here, but what am I gonna do? Can't tell him it's closing time, ask him to vacate the premises, can I? I don't know."

**ALINSKY.** I thought I knew the feeling. It connected strangely with something I heard when I was a kid in Chicago and saw an Aztec altar in the Museum, yeah, and somehow it got to me—I thought I could hear the cries of the sacrifice. That's right. Kids are impressionable, aren't they? I guess I've heard it many times since, and here it was again. I took my drink, sat down beside him, and said something profound, like… Hey, buddy, come on—maybe tomorrow's another day, hah?… things can't be as rough as all that. But of course they were. He had been everywhere—Iwo Jima, Panmunjon, Saigon… seen his buddies blown away, kept the flag waving, and now, as a recruiting sergeant, he had been driven off the campus by kids who could have been his own, as if he were some kind of ex-Nazi. So his confusion was a lot bigger than bourbon, and he sobbed and cried and had one more drink . . .And I guess I thought of all kinds of wars and how confusing things were becoming. I went up to my room and did more thinking than I wanted to about who we were and what sides we were on and how we might be something better, together. In his own way, the sergeant was showing us how fast everything was changing. And how, in their own way, a lot of people were closing their eyes to it and thrashing around in the general confusion, what with the undeclared war, the assassinations, the battles in the streets and on the campuses, kids going one way, their parents another…a lot of lashing out and backlash, a lot of trashing of the old American bedrock, a lot of, well—let's be indelicate-- crapping on the hallowed common ground. I guess I'm suggesting we have to do more, you and I, to 'bring us together' than elect...some tricky tick on the body politic who promises it at the same time he chokes on the words. I mean, all of us chewing gum would work better than that.

**JACK.** "Hey, would you buy a used car from this man?"

**JOSE.** "What are you, some kind of 'nattering nabob of negativism,' another one of those 'pusillanimous pinko pussy-footers?'"

**ALINSKY.** The games politicians—and the CEO's and the ad agencies—play. And the best we can hope for is a draw, some share in the apple pie, some stake in the action. Unless we play a few games of our own. Well, let's see if we can have some fun, all of us. Together. I've thought up a new game. Yes, that's right.

**MARTHA.** Like Monopoly?

**HATTIE.** Candyland?

**JOSE.** RISK? Penny ante? Craps?

**ALINSKY**

No. We've had all those. Something new—actually an old game, with different rules. It's a card game, easy to play, and everyone playing with a full deck. A special feature: nobody loses. Fun for everyone. I call it "Funny Money."

**JACK.** (*As MASTER OF CEREMONIES, ANNOUNCER.*) 'Well, that all sounds fascinating. I'm sure our audience would love to know just how to play, how they can get in on it. We all could use some fun these days, isn't that right, folks?'

*(Encourages applause, etc.)*

**ALINSKY.** Thank you. Well, to begin, just think of our fascination for collecting things, early on—dolls, bottlecaps, baseball cards. And then stamps. String. Matchbooks. Paperweights. Things like that.

**MARTHA.** Old newspapers. Salt and pepper shakers. Clowns, small ones.

**HATTIE.** Christmas angels . . .

**JACK.** Pennies . . .

**JOSE.** Girl friends. Wrinkles on your face. Dividend checks . . .

**ALINSKY.** Ah, yes. Pennies to dividend checks. The span of life, kids to retirees. Collectors all. Well, I'm thinking especially of a card game we used to play when I was a kid. You probably know it. "War," it was called. Not the kind we played out on the streets with sticks and stones and BB guns. Just cards. You started with the cards being dealt out, one at a time, each getting the same amount—all players are created equal. Then each turns up a card from his own pile, the high card taking the pair and adding to his stockpile. There were complexities—when each happened to play the same card, a kind of battle took place with more at stake, and the high card at that point adding the bunch, the spoils of the 'war,' to his side. And gloating over his success. On and on, till one side had all the cards. Something like that. Simple, right?

**JOSE.** Raises some questions, like...Is everyone putting his cards on the table? Is anyone getting a fast shuffle?

**ALINSKY.** Are we playing with a full deck, friends? Well, in my card game, we try to deal with such questions, with some new dealers, and fewer jokers. "Funny Money" is based on a classic utterance of one of our presidents—who may have been one of those jokers, yes: 'The business of America is business.' No, it wasn't Jefferson. But Silent Cal Coolidge had his own eloquence. Think about it. If that's our business, Americans, then do your share. You love your country? Don't mind your own business—buy American. A test of citizenship, let alone patriotism. And buy shares, become...shareholders—collect all you can, the better the player, the bigger the pile. And celebrate the national pastime all the while...

**JOSE.**
*(Singing)*
'WINSTON TASTES GOOD,
LIKE A
(Clap, clap)
CIGARETTE SHOULD!'

**HATTIE.**
*(Also)*
'CHOCK FULL O' NUTS

IS THE HEAVENLY COFFEE,
BETTER COFFEE
ROCKEFELLER'S MONEY CAN'T BUY.'

**MARTHA**
*(With a special flourish.)*
'SEE THE USA IN YOUR CHEVROLET,
AMERICA IS ASKING YOU TO CALL,
SEE THE USA IN YOUR CHEVROLET,
AMERICA'S THE GREATEST LAND OF ALL!'

**ALINSKY.** Gives you a warm feeling, doesn't it? And maybe a dividend check from General Motors. But somehow, when the cheerleading and the excitement begin to fade, you don't feel you're a part of it all.

**JOSE.** Silent partners.

**JACK.** Warming the bench.

**ALINSKY.** You're shareholders, all right, you have your shares, you're part of the All-American team, but where's the action? Well, we're in the "Funny Money" game, but we don't know it...until we get those proxy cards—you know, before the annual meeting of the shareholders, including you, where the big decisions are made about policies, attitudes to strike, directions to take. Where you get in the game, where you have a voice about how it's to be played.

**JACK.** "How the hell do I afford to take off from work?"

**MARTHA.** "Who's gonna take care of the kids?"

**ALINSKY.** Can't make it to the team meeting? No problem. Just send back your proxy cards, they'll vote your shares for you...most likely for the veteran players, the old boys and the network, or some new gang trying to become old boys.

So who's holding all the cards? We just handed 'em over. The question is, Why don't we play with a full deck? For a change.

**HATTIE.** And how does little me get to do that, she asked, with a shuffle?

**ALINSKY.** Never thought you'd ask. Well, we do the collecting, we get the cards from the other players, all over, who want to have something to say about how the game is played—about hiring practices, training and re-training programs, fairness—about pollution and the environment, overseas operations and their effect on foreign policy. Now we can begin to play. We've got a hand. We're all in the game. And it's fun.

**JACK.** *(As "emcee" again.)* "Well, there it is—'Funny Money.' I like it. Like the game Monopoly invented in the '30s, remember, folks?—get that Boardwalk and Park Place and everything else and put up those big hotels—this one looks like a game whose time has come. And I'm sure our audience will want to get in on it, won't we, folks?"

**ALINSKY.** Satisfaction guaranteed—if we all play together. Otherwise the game is fixed, and that's it. And that would be a shame, and no fun at all. You know, sometimes they, the old boys and their gang, don't play nice. Make their own rules as they go. For instance, I myself have been machine-gunned, clubbed by goons, slapped into various bastilles. Yeah. And I've heard those otherworldly voices...

**VOICES.**
"You are accused of consorting with . . . Al Capone . . ."
"Karl Marx . . ."   "Marshall Field . . ."
"Ayn Rand . . ."   "The Pope . . ."

**ALINSKY.** . . . often, all at the same time . . .

**VOICES.** "You running a Catholic front organization, aren't you?" "We Christian Soldiers and our militias do believe you to be desecrating all that is holy, son…"

**ALINSKY.** Adlai Stevenson had his own slant on things, once called me 'truly radical'—said I 'actually believe in democracy.' Now that I don't mind at all, not at all. I've been playing the game for years now – can you tell? – one way or another…with street gangs and CEO's, farm workers and students, and the rest of the home team, Native, Black, Other, and the good old middle class, the crowd that pays taxes, the 'Silent-Majority' who also feel left out sometimes. And when I wasn't benched or sent down or set upon by the moral vigilantes, I've even picked up some valuable player trophies—honorary degrees, humanitarian awards. And survived even those.

*(Segue to sprechstimme.)*

**VOICES.** "Well, what about it, after all is said and done?"

*(Echoes here.)*

**ALINSKY.**
*AND SO YOU HEAR YOUR VOICES SAY*
*WELL WHAT WAS LOST AND WHAT WAS WON*

**VOICES.**
*AND WAS IT WORTH IT AFTER ALL*
*WHEN ALL IS SAID AND DONE*

**ALINSKY.**
*EVERY DAY YOU GO TO WAR*
*EVERY DAY YOU WIN YOU LOSE*

**VOICES.**
*SOMETIMES YOU WONDER WHAT IT'S FOR*
*AND THEN YOU LEARN TO SING THE BLUES*

**ALINSKY.**
*AND EACH DAY THERE ARE FRIENDS YOU LOSE*
*AND SOME WHO'VE SIMPLY HAD ENOUGH*
*AND OTHERS WHO DESERT THE FIELD*
*WHEN LIFE DECIDES TO CALL THEIR BLUFF*

**VOICES.**
AND THERE WERE TIMES AND THERE ARE TIMES
YOU HEAR THOSE VOICES SAY SO WHAT

**ALINSKY.**
AND VICTORY BECOMES A WORD
FOR SIMPLY GIVING ALL YOU'VE GOT
AND WAS IT WORTH IT AFTER ALL
WHEN ALL IS SAID AND DONE

**MARTHA** *(AS WIFE).*
EVERY DAY A NEW CAMPAIGN
LIKE ALL THE OTHERS YOU HAVE KNOWN
EVERY NIGHT YOU LOOK AROUND
AND WONDER WHY YOU'RE ALL ALONE

*(Fade to sides, focus on ALINSKY now)*

**ALINSKY.**
AND THERE YOU TRY TO FIND YOUR LIFE
TILL IT BECOMES TOO HARD TO FIND

**THE LOVE SONG OF SAUL ALINSKY** 63

AND YOU REMEMBER IT WAS LEFT
WITH SOMEONE WHOM YOU LEFT BEHIND

BUT ALL IS FAIR IN LOVE AND WAR
UNTIL ONE DAY YOU COME TO SEE
THO' FATE MA Y NOT BE VERY KIND
YOU ARE WHAT YOU WERE MEANT TO BE

AND NO ONE SAID IT WOULD BE FAIR
JUST C'EST LA GUERRE

TOMORROW IS A NEW CAMPAIGN
SO LET IT BE AND C 'EST LA GUERRE
AND WHAT YOU LOSE YOU LEARN TO FIND
AND THAT IS WHY YOU'RE ALWAYS THERE

SO LET THEM SAY WHEN DREAMS WERE GONE
WHEN TIMES WERE LEAN HE STOOD BY YOU
HE MADE THE SCENE HE SHOWED THE WAY
HE DID THE ONLY THING TO DO

WHEN ALL IS SAID AND DONE
AND SO MUCH LEFT TO DO

JUST LET THEM SAY
WE FOUGHT OUR FIGHT
AND SOMETIMES GOT TO SAVE THE DAY
FOR ME AND YOU
AND HAD SOME FUN
WHEN ALL WAS SAID
WHEN ALL WAS DONE

AND THAT WAS ALL WE MEANT TO DO
AND IT WAS WORTH IT AFTER ALL
YES IT WAS WORTH IT AFTER ALL
TO BE WITH YOU
TO BE WITH YOU
WHEN ALL IS SAID AND DONE


And at the Pearly Gates, or thereabouts, if I had some choice, I'd ask to go to Hell. More comfortable there. You see, all my life I've been with the Have-Nots: here you're a Have-Not if you're short of money, there you're a Have-Not if you're short of virtue. I'd be asking more questions, organizing them. They're my kind of people—Hell would be Heaven for me. In the meantime, well, as Rabbi Hillel said, when you look around and fail to see a true man…or a true woman, "Be thou a man"—or "Be thou a woman"—and maybe I'll see you later. We'll have fun.

I would look forward to it.

*(Turns to exit, slowly, and fadeout.)*

www.ingramcontent.com/pod-product-compliance
Lightning Source LLC
Chambersburg PA
CBHW070650300426
44111CB00013B/2347